UNDERSTANDING THE EXECUTIVE BRANCH

INSIDE THE DEPARTMENT OF Transportation

Jennifer Peters

Enslow Publishing
101 W. 23rd Street
Suite 240
New York, NY 10011
USA
enslow.com

Published in 2019 by Enslow Publishing, LLC
101 W. 23rd Street, Suite 240, New York, NY 10011

Library of Congress Cataloging-in-Publication Data

Names: Peters, Jennifer, author. | Orr, Tamra, author.
Title: Inside the Department of Transportation / Jennifer Peters, Tamra Orr.
Description: New York : Enslow Publishing, 2019. | Series: Understanding the executive branch | Includes bibliographical references and index. | Audience: Grades 5-8.
Identifiers: LCCN 2017060953| ISBN 9780766098992 (library bound) |
ISBN 9780766099005 (pbk.)
Subjects: LCSH: United States. Department of Transportation—Juvenile literature. | Transportation and state—United States—History—Juvenile literature. | Transportation—United States—History—Juvenile literature.
Classification: LCC HE206.3 .P47 2019 | DDC 388.0973—dc23
LC record available at https://lccn.loc.gov/2017060953

Printed in the United States of America

Portions of this book originally appeared in *The Department of Transportation* by Tamra Orr.

Photo Credits: Cover, p. 1 Sheila Fitzgerald/Shutterstock.com; p. 5 Andrew F. Kazmierski/Shutterstock.com; p. 8 Bettmann/Getty Images; p. 9 Joe Raedle/Hulton Archive/Getty Images; p. 11 Richard Thornton/Shutterstock.com; pp. 14, 21 Tim Boyle/Getty Images; p. 17 Chip Somodevilla/Getty Images; p. 18 © AP Images; p. 24 Keep Smiling Photography/Shutterstock.com; p. 26 Rihardzz/Shutterstock.com; p. 29 Alexey Lesik Shutterstock.com; p. 33 Green Stock Media/Alamy Stock Photo; p. 34 Photobank gallery/Shutterstock.com; p. 36 OGI75/Shutterstock.com.

CONTENTS

INTRODUCTION

This morning, you woke up, got ready for the day, and headed to school. Unless you live really close to your school, you probably took a bus or car down a road to get there. Maybe you went over a bridge or through a tunnel. Or maybe you took a train. You could have even taken a ferryboat to school, if you live on or near an island. However you got there, your commute was made possible by the Department of Transportation (DOT). The department is responsible for building and maintaining America's roadways and for all forms of transportation, from buses and cars to subway trains, ferries, and even airplanes. Chances are, however, that you almost never see the department at work, and you probably think about it even less.

Behind the scenes, however, the transportation industry is in a constant state of motion and change, continually updating safety precautions as circumstances and our technology evolve. To guard fliers from attack, for example, airline and airport security procedures change frequently to keep up with the latest threats. Motor vehicles are constantly being redesigned and upgraded to provide a safer ride. Speed limits are raised or lowered depending on a community's competing interests in driver safety or quicker travel. The cargo loaded on to freight trains and

The Department of Transportation helps large numbers of commuters travel safely.

ships is examined to ensure that hazardous or illegal materials are not being transported throughout the country. Cities continuously search for new ways to encourage people to take buses, trains, subways, and ferries into and around the city in order to reduce car traffic and pollution. All of these modes of transportation fall under the authority of the Department of Transportation, as it seeks to improve the safety and efficiency of moving people to their desired destinations.

The Department of Transportation's mission is to develop and coordinate polices that will provide an efficient and affordable national transportation system that carefully balances the needs and interests of travelers and commuters, the environment, and national defense. The DOT is the main government agency that creates and enforces various policies and programs that directly affect how safe, quick, and efficient it is to travel within the United States. If a person hops a train, boards a bus, climbs into a car, gets on an airplane, drives onto a car ferry, or sails on a ship, the DOT had something to do with making that trip possible—from devising safety rules and regulations to installing warning signals and training transportation industry employees.

CHAPTER 1

PLANES, TRAINS, AND AUTOMOBILES

Although the Department of Transportation has only been around since 1966, when President Lyndon B. Johnson created it by signing the Department of Transportation Act, the idea of the agency has existed as long as there has been transportation—even when much of that transportation was driven by horses. In the 1800s, President Thomas Jefferson signed a law that established the first federal highway program, called the National Road. It connected the new state of Ohio with the rest of the eastern seaboard.

HIGHWAYS AND BYWAYS

At the outset of the twentieth century, as World War I (1914–1917) was looming on the horizon, President Woodrow Wilson signed into law the Federal Aid Road Act in 1916. This act established the Federal Aid Highway Program, which provided money to the various states for

President Lyndon B. Johnson (*left*) established the Department of Transportation in 1966.

building roads designed mainly for mail delivery. Throughout the 1930s, 1940s, and 1950s, additional programs were created for specific modes of transportation.

In the summer of 1961, the US Senate Committee on Commerce published a report that called for the creation of a new Department of Transportation that would oversee and regulate all of the nation's various forms of transportation. The president at the time, John F. Kennedy, responded to this proposal by instead establishing an Office of Transportation within the Housing and House Finance Agency.

The idea for an independent, powerful, cabinet-level transportation department would not go away, however. In 1965, the Federal Aviation

Agency administrator under President Lyndon B. Johnson, Najeeb E. Halaby, recommended the establishment of just such a department. In his State of the Union speech in January 1966, Johnson publicly stated that he planned to establish a DOT during his administration. By March, a bill was sent to Congress stating that "in a nation that spans a continent, transportation is the web of union" and a federal transportation department was therefore necessary.

KEEPING AMERICA RUNNING

Alan Boyd was named the nation's first secretary of transportation. He stated that the new agency would be committed to making transportation faster, more efficient, more economical, and more socially responsible.

The DOT has many functions, including conducting safety inspections of vehicles carrying goods into the United States.

New transportation policies and ideas were developed very quickly under Secretary Boyd's leadership. In January 1967, the DOT issued its first twenty federal motor vehicle safety standards. In March, the first National Highway Safety Advisory committee was formed. By April 1, Secretary Boyd had brought under one roof more than thirty transportation agencies and functions scattered throughout the government and about ninety-five thousand employees, most of whom had previously been working for the Federal Aviation Agency, the Coast Guard, and the Bureau of Public Roads.

Transportation Grinds to a Halt

John Volpe succeeded Boyd as secretary of transportation under President Richard M. Nixon. During Secretary Volpe's term, the DOT was forced to confront a number of national transportation problems. Airlines were occasionally being taken over by terrorists who took passengers hostage and hijacked planes to other countries. Hundreds of members of the Professional Air Traffic Controllers Organization (PATCO) had gone on strike. The Penn Central Railroad had declared bankruptcy.

In response to these new developments, the DOT got out in front of national policy. It headed the government's anti-hijacking program and instituted mandatory preboarding electronic scanning of airline passengers and inspection of their carry-on luggage. The DOT also helped to set up American Travel and Track, or Amtrak, a new intercity national passenger train service that would take over and expand many of Penn Central's routes.

When Nixon resigned the presidency in 1974 and was replaced by his vice president, Gerald R. Ford, William T. Coleman Jr. became the new secretary of transportation. Coleman created several reports during his brief time in office that focused on current and future transportation trends and the decisions that had to be made in order to ensure the continued health and vitality of the nation's transportation system. Some of the DOT's most important policies under Coleman included

Transportation secretary John Volpe helped develop Amtrak to take over busy train routes.

the instituting of a national 55-mile-per-hour (89-kilometer-per-hour) speed limit, the encouraging of carpooling (several people riding to work together in a single car), and making funds available for the resurfacing and restoring of the nation's interstate highways.

Restructuring

Following his defeat of Ford in the 1976 presidential election, Jimmy Carter appointed Brock Adams as secretary of transportation. Adams made a major change in the structure of the DOT when he created the Research and Special Programs Administration (RSPA), a gathering of transportation agencies that did not comfortably fit in any of the

SAFE TRAVELS

The Federal Railroad Administration's Highway-Rail Crossing Safety and Trespass Prevention Program is committed to reducing the number of car and train collisions at rail crossings, where approximately nine hundred deaths occur every year. Using the "Three E's"—education, enforcement, and engineering—the program has helped reduce the number of deaths at highway-rail crossings by 43 percent since 1994. Education involves going into schools and workplaces in communities across the country to teach about rail safety. Enforcement involves making sure that railroad employees, car drivers, and pedestrians alike obey and respect the rules governing safety on and near train tracks. The development of new technology in engineering, such as various high-tech rail barriers or train detection devices, also allows the Federal Railroad Administration to save lives.

DOT's other existing agencies. Included in the RSPA were the Transportation Systems Center and safety programs related to hazardous material transportation and oil and gas pipelines. This was the first DOT division to have been created by the department secretary rather than Congress. Secretary Adams also recommended that the Federal Highway Administration and the Urban Mass Transportation Administration be reorganized into a Surface Transportation Administration, combining federal assistance programs for the nation's highways and its cities' public transportation systems.

INTO THE MODERN ERA

President Ronald Reagan served as president of the United States throughout most of the 1980s. The first transportation secretary he appointed was Andrew L. Lewis Jr., a management consultant and political leader. Like his predecessor, Secretary Volpe, Lewis had to deal with another strike by PATCO members. In negotiations, he took a hardline position with the air traffic controllers, saying that those who did not return to work would lose their jobs. He was backed in his statements by the president. When the striking workers refused to return to work, the nation's entire force of air traffic controllers was fired and replaced. The strikers were never allowed to work as controllers again.

Lewis's successor was Elizabeth H. Dole, the first woman to serve as secretary of transportation. Her main focus was on making car travel safer. To this end, Dole tried to educate the public on the dangers of drunk driving. She also urged automakers to adopt so-called passive restraint systems, such as air bags and automatic seat belts, in their cars.

George H. W. Bush, who became president in 1989, chose Samuel K. Skinner as his secretary of transportation. Secretary Skinner's main goal was to create a national transportation policy that would maintain and expand the nation's transportation system and encourage the technologies that would create a first-class transportation system in the twenty-first century.

As part of this effort, the DOT restructured its highway, highway safety, and transit programs. Two new groups were also established within the DOT. The first of these, the Bureau of Transportation Statistics, provides transportation-related information through the collecting, studying, and publishing of transportation statistics. The second, the Office of Intermodalism, develops and coordinates federal policy on intermodal transportation (the use of two or more kinds of transportation during a single journey).

Following his defeat of George H. W. Bush in the 1992 presidential election, Bill Clinton appointed Federico Peña as his secretary of transportation. As part of a larger, government-wide attempt to improve the quality and reduce the cost of government services, Secretary Peña drafted the DOT Strategic Plan in January 1994. The plan outlined the department's mission and stated several goals for the coming years: to knit America together through an effective intermodal transportation system, to upgrade and improve transportation infrastructure (such as bridges, tunnels, airports, and highways), to promote safe and secure transportation, and to put people and the environment ahead of industry when making important transportation decisions.

TERROR IN THE SKIES

Norman Y. Mineta, President Clinton's former secretary of commerce, switched cabinet positions in 2001, when President George W. Bush asked him to head the DOT. Only eight months after Mineta took office, on September 11, 2001, al-Qaeda terrorists hijacked four American commercial jets and used them as missiles to strike the World Trade Center

After September 11, 2001, new security measures led to longer lines at airports.

in New York City and the Pentagon in Arlington, Virginia. Almost three thousand people were killed in these buildings and on the airplanes, including the plane that crashed in Shanksville, Pennsylvania, before it could reach the hijackers' intended target. As it became clear that the nation's jets were being used as weapons against it, hundreds of DOT employees had to call upon their many years of planning, training, and education in order to direct the safe grounding of every single airline flying in American airspace at the time of the attacks.

In the immediate wake of the September 11 attacks, President Bush signed into law the Aviation and Transportation Security Act, calling for increased security, not only in airports but also in other major transportation centers, such as seaports and train stations. Within the DOT, a new Transportation and Security Administration was created to increase and monitor security at important transportation sites. A year later, the cabinet-level Department of Homeland Security was created. It was designed to coordinate all of the nation's domestic security efforts and gathered together in one department many security-related agencies scattered throughout the federal government. As part of this consolidation, the DOT transferred the Transportation and Security Administration and the Coast Guard to this new cabinet office.

CHAPTER 2

LEADING THE DEPARTMENT OF TRANSPORTATION

The secretary of transportation has a very important job: supervising the creation and implementation of national transportation policy. He or she is also responsible for negotiating and implementing international transportation agreements, ensuring the safety of US airlines, enforcing airline consumer protection regulations, and developing new transportation laws. The work the secretary of transportation does impacts every single American and all of the nation's visitors. Anyone who travels anywhere within the borders of America is being kept safe by the work of the secretary and the other employees of the Department of Transportation. To learn more about how the DOT keeps people safe, it's important to look at some of the most impressive men and women to have led the department so far.

Appointed by President Donald Trump, Elaine Chao is the eighteenth secretary of transportation.

A REAL ORIGINAL

The very first person to have the title of secretary of transportation was a man named Alan Stephenson Boyd. When appointed by President Lyndon B. Johnson in 1967, Boyd had already gained extensive experience in transportation. Not only was he the former Civil Aeronautics Board chairman and undersecretary of commerce for transportation, he had also served as the chairman of the Florida Railroad and Public Utilities Commission. Secretary Boyd was faced with a different kind of challenge in his new job, however. This time he was in charge of creating a brand-new cabinet-level department,

Brock Adams (*far left*) mandated that all cars include either air bags or automatic seat belts.

building it up from scratch while paying careful attention to Congress's recommendations.

During Boyd's two years in office, the department issued the very first national safety and federal motor vehicle standards. President Johnson increased the secretary's responsibilities when he transferred the Urban Mass Transportation Administration from the Department of Housing and Urban Development to the newly formed DOT. In addition to this, Boyd also concentrated on modernizing airports and updating air traffic control requirements. By shaping the new DOT and establishing its responsibilities and standards, Secretary Boyd created a roadmap for those who would follow in his footsteps as leader of this important department.

American Transportation in Crisis

The third secretary of transportation was a forty-five-year-old man named Claude Stout Brinegar. He approached the position with a strong background in business and economics. He had served as the senior vice president of the Union Oil Company, and held a Ph.D. in economic research from Stanford University.

During his term, Brinegar was confronted with the energy crisis of 1973 and 1974, which was caused by an oil embargo imposed on the United States by the Arab-dominated Organization of Petroleum Exporting Countries (OPEC). The Arab nations in OPEC were angered at the United States for its support of Israel during the Yom Kippur War, in which Israel beat back a surprise attack led by Egypt and Syria. The result was a severe shortage of the imported oil and gas on which the United States heavily relies. The energy crisis called the nation's attention to the impact of transportation—especially car travel—on energy consumption.

In response to the energy crisis, President Nixon and Secretary Brinegar put into place several new pieces of transportation and energy policy. Nixon launched Project Independence, which called for American energy self-sufficiency by 1980. As part of this effort, Nixon authorized the construction of an oil pipeline that would carry two million barrels of crude oil from Alaska's northern oil fields to its ice-free port of Valdez for shipment to the continental United States. Together, Nixon and Brinegar promoted carpooling and helped institute the national 55-mile-per-hour (89-km-per-hour) speed limit, which helped reduce fuel use.

Crash-Test Dummies

In 1978, the National Highway Traffic Safety Administration began its New Car Assessment Program. This program was designed to give car buyers reliable information about how safe specific models of cars are. In order to provide this information, the program ran a series of front- and side-crash tests on many of the cars sold in the United States. The results of the program's crash tests also often encourage automakers to make safer cars, if only so they will not receive the bad publicity that comes with having a car fail the test. The vehicles chosen for the crash tests are those that are expected to be sold in great numbers and those that have been redesigned or received new safety features. For testing frontal collisions, crash-test dummies are placed in driver and front passenger seats and wear seat belts. Vehicles are crashed into a fixed barrier at 35 miles per hour (56 km/h), which is equivalent to a head-on collision between two similar vehicles each moving at 35 miles per hour. Instruments measure the force of impact to each dummy's head, chest, and legs. The resulting information indicates a belted person's chances of suffering a serious injury in the event of a crash. For testing side-impact collisions, crash-test dummies are placed in driver and driver's side rear passenger seats wearing seat belts. This test represents an intersection-type collision with a 3,015-pound (1,368-kilogram) barrier moving at 38.5 miles per hour (62 km/h) into a standing vehicle.

Crash and Burn?

When President Jimmy Carter appointed Brockman Adams to the position of secretary of transportation, he chose someone with a high degree of political experience. Adams had already served six terms in the House of Representatives from the state of Washington, and there had been rumors that he was a strong candidate for the job of Speaker of the House. During his years in the House, Adams was considered to be an authority on transportation issues. He had been the principal author of the legislation that had taken the bankrupt northeastern rail lines and converted them into the profitable Conrail system.

In his two years with the DOT, Adams had a major impact on the safety designs of motor vehicles. Through his dedication, every car manufacted in the United States was required to have either air bags or automatic seat belts installed. He announced new fuel economy standards and demanded that automobile manufacturers make design changes that would result in smaller, lighter cars that would use less fuel per mile driven.

SAFE AND SOUND

Norman Mineta and the DOT took on expanded responsibilities after the attacks of September 11.

President Ronald Reagan appointed Elizabeth Hanford Dole to be the eighth secretary of the DOT. She was the first woman to ever hold the position.

Dole spent her two terms as secretary focusing on many safety-related issues, especially air bag usage. She helped establish deadlines for installing these safety devices in vehicles and created a variety of incentives to encourage motor vehicle manufacturers to equip cars with these life-saving bags. In addition, she emphasized increasing seat belt usage by the general public and encouraged the individual states to pass laws requiring them. Perhaps she is best known, however, for what came to be called the "Dole brake light." It was her idea and her efforts that resulted in rear-window brake lights being installed in various motor vehicles starting in the mid-1980s.

A NEW ERA OF TERROR

On January 25, 2001, Norman Yoshio Mineta became the fourteenth secretary of transportation. Mineta was serving as secretary of transportation when the World Trade Center and the Pentagon were attacked by terrorists flying hijacked American airplanes on September 11, 2001. On that day, Mineta, along with DOT managers and air traffic controllers, performed the enormous task of bringing every airplane flying in American airspace back down to the ground safely and shutting down the entire nation's aviation system in less than two hours.

In the wake of September 11, Mineta's job and the DOT's responsibilities increased greatly. The secretary helped draft the new Aviation and Transportation Security Act, a law designed to strengthen security throughout the country's airports. Under the terms of this law, Mineta helped create the Transportation Security Administration (TSA), which was initially housed within the DOT. It was later transferred to the newly created Department of Homeland Security.

CHAPTER 3

HOW THE DEPARTMENT OF TRANSPORTATION WORKS

There are eleven agencies that make up the DOT. Each one has specific responsibilities and is tasked with managing a different part of Americans' lives on the road, on the water, or in the air. Together, these agencies within the DOT help keep travelers safe and ensure that Americans are able to get from point A to point B with as little effort as possible.

BUREAU OF TRANSPORTATION STATISTICS (BTS)

Just as its name implies, the Bureau of Transportation Statistics (BTS) focuses on compiling and analyzing various statistics regarding the different forms of transportation. It collects enormous amounts of data, or

The Federal Highway Administration (FHWA) oversees the maintenance and repair of highways, roads, bridges, and tunnels.

facts and figures, and publishes it in order to educate politicians and the public about potential decisions relating to transportation issues. Along with the Bureau of the Census, the BTS also helps identify exactly where freight and people travel and by what kind of transportation.

FEDERAL AVIATION ADMINISTRATION (FAA)

The FAA is responsible for the safety of civil aviation, or planes that non-military passengers fly. The FAA enforces the regulations and minimum standards relating to the production, operation, and maintenance of aircraft. In addition to drafting the rules governing air traffic, the FAA controls the nation's air traffic by maintaining and supervising a network of airport towers, air route traffic control centers, and flight service stations. It builds and installs equipment that makes flying safer and easier, such as radar facilities, voice and data communications equipment, and computer systems.

The FAA also exchanges aeronautical information with its counterparts in other countries.

Federal Highway Administration (FHWA)

Not only does the Federal Highway Administration ensure that federal highways, roads, bridges, and tunnels stay safe, it helps repair things when disaster strikes. Whether earthquakes shatter the roads or floods engulf them, for example, the FHWA arrives on the scene in order to make those emergency repairs. The FHWA has two basic programs. First, there is the Federal-Aid Highway Program, which focuses on providing federal funds to the states in order to build and improve the National Highway System, as well as urban and rural roads and bridges. The FHWA's Federal Lands Highway Program exists to provide access to places like Native American reservations, national forests and parks, and other public lands.

Federal Motor Carrier Safety Administration (FMCSA)

The FMCSA's primary aim is to do everything it can to decrease the number of accidents and injuries from crashes involving motor carriers—trucks or buses. In order to do this, the FMCSA creates and enforces federal rules that govern carrier safety. It establishes safe operating requirements for professional truck drivers, their vehicles, and their equipment. In addition, the FMCSA enforces rules that try to ensure the safe transport of hazardous materials from one place to another.

To ensure that bus and truck drivers in the United States are properly trained and educated, the FMCSA administers both the Commercial Driver's License Program and the New Entrant Safety Assurance Process. It also sponsors a federal grant program called the Motor Carrier Safety Assistance Program, which supplies the states with the financial assistance they need in order to conduct roadside inspections of trucks and buses and reviews of driver performance and licensing.

The Federal Motor Carrier Safety Administration (FMCSA) monitors the operations of trucks and buses as well as the transport of hazardous materials.

The Performance and Registration Information Systems Management is another FMCSA program that monitors the safety records of carriers and their drivers.

Federal Railroad Administration (FRA)

The FRA was first established in 1966 in order to ensure and improve the safety of railroads through both maintenance of the nation's train tracks and trains and education of rail industry employees. FRA safety inspectors make sure that rail companies are obeying federally established rail safety standards. In addition, research and development tests are used to enhance the rail system as a national transportation resource. For example, the so-called bullet trains—trains that can travel at speeds greater than 100 miles per hour (161 km/h)—are the sort of new technology being carefully studied by the FRA. The administration also leads public education campaigns designed to warn against the extreme dangers of driving across rail crossings or walking along train tracks.

Can I Fly with This?

In an effort to be more approachable to help citizens figure out what they can bring along when they fly, the TSA runs an Instagram account that showcases all the strange objects people pack when they travel. The account shares images of things that have been allowed—like Thanksgiving pies, piñatas, and inflatable T-rex costumes—and others that were definitely not. Among the items TSA agents have found passengers trying to sneak onboard are giant tubs of gunpowder, grenades that look like baseballs, throwing stars, and flare guns. Along with the Instagram account, the TSA also runs an AskTSA Twitter account so anyone can ask the agency if they can bring their goodies with them on their next trip.

Federal Transit Administration (FTA)

The FTA's mission is to develop and improve systems of mass transit for cities nationwide. Mass transit refers to the systems of vehicles—trains, subways, buses, ferries—that carry large groups of people to and throughout large cities. The FTA's staff helps to plan, build, and operate these systems and places an emphasis on passenger affordability, accessibility, and convenience. Detailed data and records are kept on each mode of mass transit. This information is shared with those who must make transit decisions, such as whether to expand bus lines or add subway cars based on heavy ridership.

Maritime Administration (MARAD)

The MARAD is mainly concerned with promoting the development of a strong US merchant marine. The merchant marine is simply all of the nation's commercial, nonmilitary ships that are used to carry goods on the United States' oceans, rivers, and lakes. In times of war or other national emergency, the merchant marine may be called upon to assist the armed forces by lending their boats and crews for military purposes, such as the transport of equipment or soldiers. MARAD also ensures that the United States maintains enough shipbuilding and repair services, efficient ports, effective water and land transportation systems, and reserve ships for use in any national emergencies.

National Highway Traffic Safety Administration (NHTSA)

Established in 1970, the NHTSA is the primary DOT division responsible for reducing the deaths, injuries, and economic losses that often accompany motor vehicle crashes. It carries out this mission by setting and enforcing safety performance standards for motor vehicle

The Maritime Administration (MARAD) regulates all commercial ships that carry goods within the United States. These ships are collectively known as the merchant marine.

equipment and offering grants to state and local governments for the development and installation of local highway safety programs.

The NHTSA also investigates safety defects in vehicles, enforces fuel economy standards, helps communities keep drunk drivers off the road, promotes the use of seat belts and child safety seats, and provides important safety information to consumers about traffic issues. This is the department that issues recalls when something is found to be wrong with a vehicle. It also performs crash tests on all types of vehicles to learn how they fare in an accident. The results of these tests are published, offering car buyers valuable information about which cars are the safest.

RESEARCH AND SPECIAL PROGRAMS ADMINISTRATION (RSPA)

The RSPA has been in existence since 1977 and was initially designed to administer the programs that did not easily fit into the other DOT divisions. Today the RSPA focuses primarily on developing new technology that will improve the safety and efficiency with which people and cargo are transported throughout the entire world and with the help of all available forms of transportation. As part of this mission, the RSPA is charged with reducing the risk of the transportation of hazardous goods, such as the shipping of toxic chemicals in tanker trucks or the delivery of oil through pipelines. By offering training and technical assistance, the RSPA also makes sure that communities are prepared for any transportation-related emergencies that may occur, such as a chemical spill on a local highway.

SAINT LAWRENCE SEAWAY DEVELOPMENT CORPORATION (SLSDC)

The SLSDC works together with the Saint Lawrence Seaway Authority of Canada to provide safe and efficient passage for commercial and noncommercial ships traveling throughout the Great Lakes and along the Saint Lawrence Seaway to or from the Atlantic Ocean. This waterway is 2,342 miles (3,769 km) long and includes canals, dams, and locks in the Saint Lawrence River, along with connecting channels between the Great Lakes. It was opened in 1959. The SLSDC is responsible for operations safety, vessel inspections, traffic control, and navigation aids along the Saint Lawrence Seaway. It also helps develop trade opportunities that benefit everyone involved in seaway trade, from ports and shippers to receivers and consumers.

Surface Transportation Board (STB)

Established in 1996, the STB is responsible for making sure that the transportation services provided by railroads, certain trucking and moving companies, intercity buses, and ocean shipping companies are both safe and fairly priced. Although it is housed within the DOT, it is considered independent.

Chapter 4

Twenty-First-Century Travel Problems

As the population of America has grown, so have the country's transportation needs. To keep up with the growing demand for planes, trains, and automobiles, the DOT has helped fund research into new transportation options, better fuel types, and faster methods of travel. But it isn't done yet. As we head into the future, the DOT will need to increase its efforts to make sure Americans can get around quickly and efficiently even with more people traveling through the country.

Up in the Sky

The future of flight will be determined by what new planes can be made to do and what new materials will go into their construction. Scientists at the Langley Research Center in Virginia have been working on a program

As more people travel around the United States, the Department of Transportation must continue to research and innovate to keep methods of transporation efficient and safe.

they call the Morphing Project. To morph is to undergo a major change of some kind. Early studies in this project are focusing on a new kind of material that would be used in the construction of airplane wings. This high-tech material would allow the wings to flex or bend on command. Because the material would allow them to be fully adjustable, the wings would not have any mechanical flaps, which would save fuel and money.

RIDING THE RAILS

Train designs will be undergoing a number of changes, too. A new type of train being tested in Britain tilts as it goes around corners, keeping it fully

New developments in airplane technology, like flexible, fully adjustable wings, could save a dramatic amount of fuel and money for airlines.

upright and level no matter how steeply the ground beneath it slopes. This allows the train to maintain speeds of 140 miles per hour (225 km/h) or so even when it is not traveling on a straight stretch of track.

Another new train design that is creating a lot of interest and enthusiasm is the "maglev" train, or magnetic levitation train. Instead of the cars being outfitted with steel wheels that ride on the tracks, the maglev train features magnets under its cars. A magnetic field created by magnetized coils in the guideway—the maglev equivalent of train tracks—floats the train above the ground and pushes and pulls it along at very high speeds. In some trials, maglev trains have ranged between 260 and 340 miles per hour (418 and 547 km/h). Because there are no wheels making contact with the track, there is no friction to slow the train down or require a large, fossil fuel–burning engine. In fact, the magnetic field powers the train, so there is no need for either fuel or an engine on a maglev train. Already popular in Japan, the DOT has given millions of dollars to seven different companies to try to develop the best system for America's needs.

KEEPING ALL TRAVELERS SAFE

Pedestrian and bicyclist deaths represent about 15 percent of all roadway-related deaths each year. For this reason, the Federal Highway Administration sponsors the Pedestrian and Bicyclist Safety Program, which is designed to reduce these deaths. For example, in an area known for its pedestrian and bicyclist deaths, representatives of the Pedestrian and Bicyclist Safety Program might recommend the building of sidewalks, the installation of street lamps, and the addition of crosswalks and traffic lights. It may also urge pedestrians and bicyclists to wear bright or reflective clothing when walking and riding after dark.

HITTING THE ROAD

Perhaps the transportation mode that will require the most attention and creative problem solving in the coming years will be motor vehicles. Traffic congestion worsens from year to year. Each year, American commuters collectively spend 6.9 billion hours sitting in rush-hour traffic jams. While once the solution seemed simple—build more roads—there is no longer enough room left to do that. Instead, researchers at the DOT and other organizations are trying to find ways to make the most of the highways that already exist and to encourage the use of the mass transit and carpooling.

Driverless cars are also being explored. The idea is that computer-controlled cars would be better at keeping traffic flowing and protecting

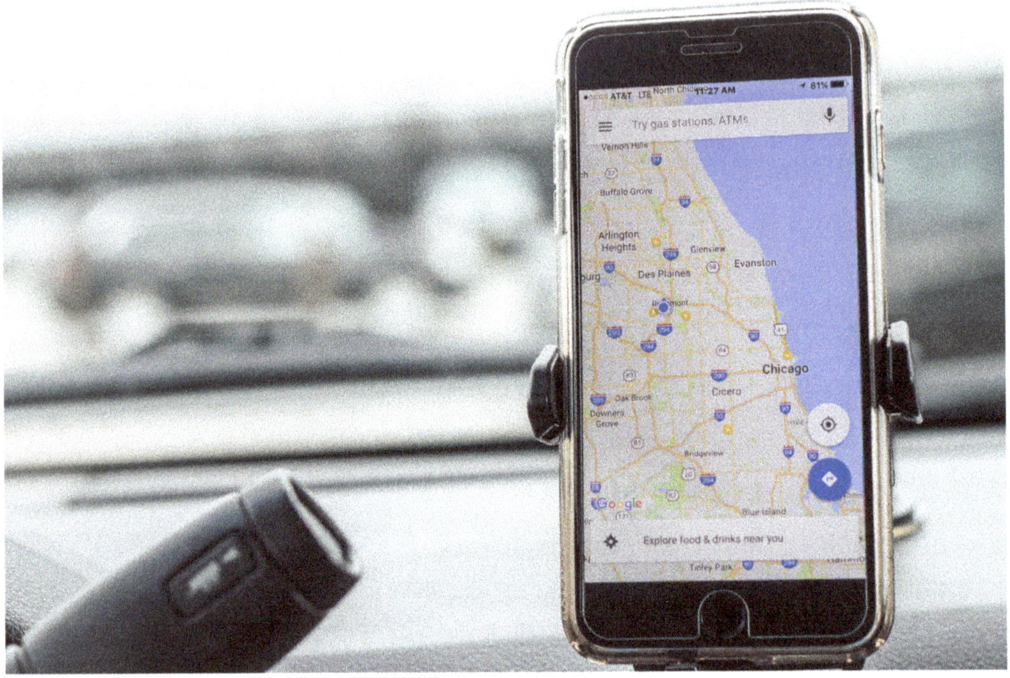

While GPS was a major improvement in mapping technology for drivers, companies like Google and Tesla are looking ahead to building driverless cars run by computers.

passengers, since so many of the problems drivers encounter are caused by other drivers. In addition to running the car by computer, driverless cars will also rely on sensors in the roadway to help them maintain good driving practices and keep traffic moving smoothly. Google is currently testing its driverless car system in California, and tech mogul Elon Musk, CEO of the American automaker Tesla, believes driverless cars will be available by 2019.

Conclusion

Since Americans got the first horseless carriage—what we now call a car—they've been excitedly traveling to and fro on America's highways and byways, crisscrossing the country for business and pleasure and using every mode of transportation available to them. But they can only do that thanks to the work of the DOT.

More people are now traveling by car, by bus, by train, and by plane than ever before, making traffic slow down whether it's on the ground, in the sky, or over the water. And that means people may be trying to go places, but they aren't always getting there. It's up to the Department of Transportation to fix that. In some instances, that may mean building more roads or vehicles, or finding new ways to monitor travel in order to help keep travelers moving. It could mean developing new kinds of transportation technology to help commuters better manage their time and travel, or it could mean finding ways to convince people to stop driving and pushing them toward other modes of transportation.

Some day, we may see the DOT promoting flying cars or teleportation, but until our real-life science matches our science-fiction fantasy of futuristic travel, the DOT and the secretary will need to work with the technology available to them to keep America's travelers on the go.

Chronology

1916 President Woodrow Wilson signs into law the Federal Aid Road Act.

1961 US Senate Committee on Commerce publishes a report that calls for the creation of a new Department of Transportation that will oversee and regulate all of the nation's various forms of transportation.

January 12, 1966 A cabinet-level Department of Transportation is announced for the first time in President Lyndon B. Johnson's State of the Union speech.

October 15, 1966 The Department of Transportation Act is signed into law by President Lyndon B. Johnson.

1966 Federal Railroad Administration is created in order to ensure and improve the safety of the nation's railroads through maintenance and education of rail industry employees.

1967–1969 Alan S. Boyd serves as the first secretary of transportation.

January 31, 1967 DOT issues its first twenty federal motor vehicle safety standards.

April 1, 1967 The new cabinet-level DOT opens for its first official day of business.

June 6, 1967 The National Traffic Safety Agency and the National Highway Safety Agency are merged to become the National Highway Safety Bureau.

July 1, 1968 The Urban Mass Transportation Administration is established.

1969–1973 John A. Volpe serves as secretary of transportation.

September 11, 1970 President Nixon orders the DOT to lead the government's anti-hijacking program.

October 13, 1970 President Nixon signs the Federal Railroad Safety Act, increasing the DOT's role in overseeing the safe operation of the nation's railroads.

October 15, 1970 Congress passes the National Railroad Passenger Safety Act, creating Amtrak, designed to improve the nation's intercity rail passenger service.

December 31, 1970 National Highway Traffic Safety Administration is established to reduce the deaths, injuries, and economic losses that often accompany motor vehicle crashes.

March 9, 1972 The Transportation Safety Institute is established.

January 5, 1973 The FAA begins preboarding electronic screening of all passengers and inspection of their carry-on baggage.

1973–1975 Claude S. Brinegar serves as secretary of transportation.

April 5, 1974 After the energy crisis caused by the Arab oil embargo, the federal government orders to reduce maximum highway speed limits to 55 miles per hour.

December 13, 1974 Still in the middle of an energy crisis, the DOT launches a nationwide campaign to encourage carpooling.

1975–1975 John W. Barnum serves as secretary of transportation.

1975–1977 William T. Coleman Jr. serves as secretary of transportation

1977–1979 Brockman Adams serves as secretary of transportation.

June 6, 1977 Adams announces new fuel economy standards that are intended to create smaller and lighter cars.

September 23, 1977 Research and Special Programs Administration is created to develop new technology that will improve the safety and efficiency with which people and cargo are transported throughout the entire world.

November 6, 1978 The Surface Transportation Assistance Act is signed into law, consolidating federal financial assistance programs for highways and public transportation

1978 National Highway Traffic Safety Administration begins its New Car Assessment Program, designed to give car buyers reliable information about how safe specific models are. To provide this information, the program runs a series of front and side crash tests on many of the cars sold in the United States.

1979–1979 W. Graham Clayton Jr. serves as secretary of transportation.

July 30, 1979 The Office of Small and Disadvantaged Business Utilization is established.

1979–1981 Neil E. Goldschmidt serves as secretary of transportation.

August 5, 1981 President Ronald Reagan fires almost twelve thousand striking air traffic controllers.

August 6, 1981 The Maritime Administration is transferred from the Commerce Department to the DOT.

December 29, 1981 President Reagan signs into law the Federal Aid Highway Act, which provides funds for the resurfacing, restoring, and reconstructing of the Interstate Highway system.

1981–1983 Andrew L. "Drew" Lewis Jr serves as secretary of transportation.

1983–1987 Elizabeth H. Dole serves as secretary of transportation.

October 13, 1983 Secretary Dole orders the installation of eye-level brake lights on rear windshields of new cars.

July 17, 1984 President Reagan signs into law legislation that establishes the national minimum drinking age of twenty-one, in part to cut down on drunk-driving deaths. States that don't comply with the new law will lose their federal highway funds.

August 27, 1986 The Omnibus Diplomatic Security and Antiterrorism Act is signed into law. The DOT must issue reports on security at foreign and domestic ports.

1987–1989 James H. Burnley serves as secretary of transportation.

1989–1991 Samuel K. Skinner serves as secretary of transportation.

February 25, 1990 Smoking is prohibited on nearly all domestic flights. The only exceptions are flights to Alaska and Hawaii that last more than six hours.

October 15, 1990 President George H. W. Bush renames the National System of Interstate and Defense Highways as the Dwight D. Eisenhower System of Interstate and Defense Highways. President Eisenhower created the system in 1956.

1991–1992 James B. Busey IV serves as secretary of transportation.

1992–1993 Andrew H. Card Jr. serves as secretary of transportation.

1993–1997 Federico F. Peńa serves as secretary of transportation.

June 8, 1993 The National Roadcheck is held in the United States, Mexico, and Canada.

February 3, 1994 The DOT issues alcohol and drug testing rules for over seven million employees who conduct safety-sensitive jobs in the transportation industry.

April 21, 1994 The Office of Motor Carrier Safety creates its "Share the Road" campaign, which is designed to teach motorists how to drive safely on highways that are also occupied by large trucks.

October 7–9, 1994 The DOT holds its first technology fair in Washington, DC.

1994 Secretary of Transportation Peńa drafts the DOT Strategic Plan, which outlines the department's mission and several goals for the next few years.

January 1, 1996 Surface Transportation Board is created to make sure that the transportation services provided by railroads, certain trucking and moving companies, intercity buses, and ocean shipping companies are both safe and fairly priced.

1997–2001 Rodney E. Slater serves as secretary of transportation.

2001–2001 Mortimer L. Downey serves as secretary of transportation.

2001–2006 Norman Y. Mineta serves as secretary of transportation.

September 11, 2001 Al-Qaeda terrorists hijack four American commercial jets and use them as missiles to strike the World Trade Center towers in New York City and the Pentagon in Arlington, Virginia. The fourth plane crashes in a field in Shanksville, Pennsylvania.

November 19, 2001 President George W. Bush signs the Aviation and Transportation Security Act into law, creating the DOT's

Transportation Security Administration, which is tasked with increasing security at major public transportation hubs.

March 1, 2003 The Department of Homeland Security takes over the US Coast Guard and the Transportation Security Administration, two departments that previously belonged to the DOT.

2006–2009 Mary E. Peters serves as secretary of transportation.

2009–2013 Ray L. LaHood serves as secretary of transportation.

2013–2017 Anthony R. Foxx serves as secretary of transportation.

2017–2017 Michael Huerta serves as secretary of transportation.

2017–Present Elaine Chao serves as secretary of transportation.

BIBLIOGRAPHY

Abuelsamid, Sam. "U.S. Department of Transportation Issues Simplified Automated Driving Guidelines." *Forbes*, September 12, 2017. https://www.forbes.com/sites/samabuelsamid/2017/09/12/u-s-department-of-transportation-issues-simplified-automated-driving-guidelines/#340fe9cf41fa.

AllGov. "Department of Transportation (DOT)." http://www.allgov.com/departments/department-oftransportation?detailsDepartmentID=578.

American Public Transportation Association. "About APTA." http://www.apta.com/about/governance/Pages/default.aspx.

Bogage, Jacob. "Yes, Stricter Driving Laws Really Do Make Us Safer." *Washington Post*, July 14, 2016. https://www.washingtonpost.com/news/wonk/wp/2016/07/14/yes-stricter-driving-laws-really-do-make-us-safer/?utm_term=.0d10740725ef.

Freed, Jamie, and David Shepardson. "Airlines Get Ready for New U.S. Security Rules from Thursday." Reuters, October 24, 2017. https://www.reuters.com/article/us-usa-airlines-security/airlines-get-ready-for-new-u-s-security-rules-from-thursday-idUSKBN1CT2GE.

National Transportation Safety Board. "History of the National Transportation Safety Board." https://www.ntsb.gov/about/history/Pages/default.aspx.

US Department of Transportation. "About Us." https://www.transportation.gov/mission/about-us.

US Department of Transportation: Federal Railroad Administration. "About FRA." https://www.fra.dot.gov/Page/P0002.

GLOSSARY

bill A draft of a law presented to a legislature and submitted to a vote.

cabinet A council of the chief advisors of a head of state.

cabinet-level department A government office headed by a key advisor to a head of state, such as the president of the United States.

cargo Goods carried on a mode of transportation.

economy The flow of money within a country, state, region, city, town, or household.

embargo A cutting-off of trade.

federal The central governing authority in a nation made up of several states or territories.

hazardous Something that is risky or dangerous.

incentive Something that motivates one to do something.

infrastructure The support system of a city or country that allows it to function, such as the sanitation system, power plants, water pipelines, bridges, tunnels, highways, and railways.

legislation Proposed rules created by a decision-making body, like the US Congress or a town council.

negotiation A discussion aimed at reaching an agreement.

Organization of Petroleum Exporting Countries (OPEC) A cartel of major oil-exporting countries established in 1960 to control the pricing and production of oil.

statistics Information that is collected, counted, analyzed, and presented publicly; information that is collected so understanding of a certain issue can be increased.

transportation The means of traveling from one place to another.

FURTHER READING

BOOKS

Humes, Edward. *Door to Door: The Magnificent, Maddening, Mysterious World of Transportation*. New York, NY: HarperCollins, 2017.

Petroski, Henry. *The Road Taken: The History and Future of America's Infrastructure*. New York, NY: Bloomsbury USA, 2017.

Swift, Earl. *The Big Roads: The Untold Stories of the Engineers, Visionaries, and Trailblazers Who Created the American Superhighways*. New York, NY: Houghton Mifflin Harcourt, 2012.

Wolmar, Christian. *The Great Railroad Revolution: The History of Trains in America*. New York, NY: PublicAffairs, 2013.

WEBSITES

Bureau of Transportation Statistics

www.bts.gov

The BTS provides information that is used to shape transportation policy, investments, and research across the United States and abroad.

Federal Aviation Administration

www.faa.gov

The mission of the FAA is to provide the safest, most efficient aerospace system in the world.

Federal Highway Administration

www.fhwa.dot.gov

The FHA is a leader in shaping the future of highway transportation in the United States.

Federal Motor Carrier Safety Administration
www.fmcsa.dot.gov
The mission of the FMCSA is to reduce crashes, injuries, and fatalities involving large trucks and buses.

Federal Railroad Administration
www.fra.dot.gov
The FRA's mission is to enable the safe, reliable, and efficient movement of people and goods in America.

Federal Transit Administration
www.transit.dot.gov
The FTA provides financial and technical assistance to local public transit systems and also oversees safety measures and helps develop next-generation technology research.

National Highway Traffic Safety Administration
www.nhtsa.gov
Through enforcing vehicle performance standards and partnerships with state and local governments, NHTSA reduces deaths, injuries, and economic losses from motor vehicle crashes.

INDEX